This Candlewick book belongs to

Tatman

I pledge allegiance

The Pledge of Allegiance, with commentary by

BILL MARTIN JR and MICHAEL SAMPSON

illustrated by

CHRIS RASCHKA

CANDLEWICK PRESS
CAMBRIDGE, MASSACHUSETTS

1

pledge

A pledge is a promise.

allegiance   to

Allegiance is loyalty.

the flag

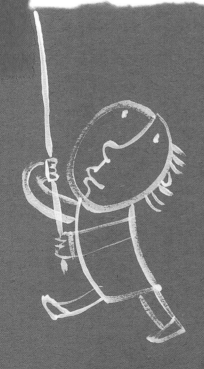

A flag is a symbol that stands for
a place, a thing, or an idea.

of

Making a promise to a flag usually means the same thing as making a promise to whatever the flag stands for.

Each state has its own name,

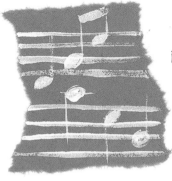

its own song,

bird,

and flower,

the United States

its own favorite food,

some
of
its
own
laws,

and even its own flag!

of

The United States is one country made up of
fifty states and several territories.

America

America is a big
body of land made
up of two continents:
North America and
South America.
All but one of the
U.S. states are part
of North America.
The island state of
Hawaii is in the
south Pacific Ocean.

Why our flag isn't orange and pink:

Red is for courage.

White is for purity and innocence.

Blue is for loyalty and fairness.

In 1818, lawmakers decided that the U.S. flag would have thirteen stripes for the original thirteen colonies, and a star for every state.

and to

Wouldn't they be surprised to learn that the flag would one day have fifty stars!

the republic

The United States of America is a republic, which means
that we the people elect leaders who make our laws.

Things you can do while saying the pledge:

- Stand at attention.
- Look at an American flag.
- Place your right hand over your heart.
- If you have a cap or a hat on, it is polite to take it off and place it over your heart.

for which it stands,

Did you know that the Pledge of Allegiance was written especially for children? It was written by a man named Francis Bellamy.

Mr. Bellamy published his poem in 1892 in the children's magazine *The Youth's Companion*.

That year, twelve million students said the pledge together as one voice to celebrate the 400th anniversary of Columbus's arrival in the Americas.

one

nation

Our states and territories have bonded together to form one nation.
One nation means one country.

People of many different races, cultures, and faiths call America their home.

under

God,

Many people believe that a democracy is a reflection of how God thinks —
every single person is important.

indivisible,

Indivisible means unbreakable —
our country cannot be split into separate parts.

No matter how much we might disagree about some things, we all agree on one thing: we are strongest when we stick together and help each other out.

with

liberty

Liberty is freedom.

and

Every person who lives in this country has a right
to be free and to make his or her own choices.

justice

Justice is fairness.

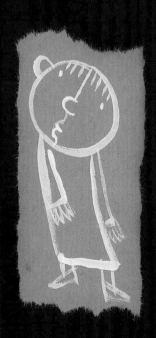

for

All Americans have the right to be treated fairly by our laws.

all.

I pledge allegiance to the flag of the United States of America and to the republic for which it stands, one nation under God, indivisible, with liberty and justice for all.

The United States of America is a country built on some big ideas —
unity and variety, fairness and freedom, creativity and equality.
America grows and changes as the world changes, but we always
try to hold on to the principles of "liberty and justice for all."

The American flag is a symbol of who we are as a people. The flag
stands for our history, our inventions, our music, sports, literature, faith,
and the hopes and feelings of the American people — people like . . .

you!

To the children of America
and their love for Old Glory
B. M. & M. S.

To my parents, who taught
me to think freely
C. R.

First paperback edition 2004

The Library of Congress has cataloged the hardcover edition as follows:

Bellamy, Francis.
[Pledge of Allegiance to the Flag]
I pledge allegiance : the Pledge of Allegiance : with commentary /
by Bill Martin Jr and Michael Sampson ;
illustrated by Chris Raschka. — 1st ed.
p.   cm.
Summary: Divides the Pledge of Allegiance into words and phrases
in order to define its meaning.
ISBN 0-7636-1648-6 (hardcover)
1. Bellamy, Francis. Pledge of Allegiance to the Flag — Juvenile
literature. 2. Flags — United States — Juvenile literature. [1. Pledge
of Allegiance. 2. Flags — United States.] I. Martin, Bill, date.
II. Sampson, Michael R. III. Raschka, Christopher, ill. IV. Title.
JC346.B45 2002
323.6'5'0973 — dc21   2002276812

ISBN 0-7636-2527-2 (paperback)

10 9 8 7 6 5 4 3 2 1

Printed in the United States of America

This book was typeset in Badger.
The illustrations were done in ink and torn paper.

Candlewick Press
2067 Massachusetts Avenue
Cambridge, Massachusetts 02140

visit us at www.candlewick.com

BILL MARTIN JR, a literary expert and the author of more than 300 books—including the beloved classic *Brown Bear, Brown Bear, What Do You See?* illustrated by Eric Carle—was named one of the "Greats of the Century" by the International Reading Association. "I think the Pledge of Allegiance is the most beautiful chain of language I know," Dr. Martin says. "It's a miracle that children can even recite the Pledge of Allegiance with its sophisticated and complex language, yet they jump right in." Bill Martin Jr lives in Texas.

MICHAEL SAMPSON says, "I have a deep love for this country and the Pledge—I get goose bumps every time I recite it. This book makes the Pledge come alive for kids with language they can understand." Dr. Sampson is the author of many books for children and of books for adults about literacy. He lives in Texas.

CHRIS RASCHKA is the illustrator of many picture books, including the concrete poetry anthology *A Poke in the I* edited by Paul B. Janeczko, a *New York Times* Best Illustrated Children's Book, and is the author-illustrator of the Caldecott Honor Book *Yo! Yes?* Chris Raschka says, "My parents have always respectfully refused to recite the Pledge of Allegiance—for religious reasons and reasons of personal experience. That's why I was drawn to this project. In America, we each have the freedom to choose, including the freedom to choose whether or not to say the Pledge." He lives in New York City with his wife and son.